MEMORIES
OF
DUDLEY

ALTON DOUGLAS
DENNIS MOORE
ADDITIONAL RESEARCH BY JO DOUGLAS

© 1989 Alton Douglas, Dennis Moore, Jo Douglas
© 1999 Alton and Jo Douglas. 4th Impression
© 2007 Alton and Jo Douglas. 5th Impression
ISBN 10: 1-85858-135-4
ISBN 13: 978-1-85858-135-4
Published by Brewin Books Ltd, Doric House,
56 Alcester Road, Studley, Warwickshire B80 7LG
Printed at Cromwell Press Limited, Great Britain.

CONTENTS

INTRODUCTION

Dudley was first recorded about the time of the Domesday Book (1083-1086), although an important manor existed there before the Norman Conquest. The first mention of the town spells it Dudelei, followed in the 13th century by Duddelie and Duddleye. The Anglo-Saxon surname of Dudda was quite a common one and whilst we may never know who this particular Dudda was, he must have lived nearby and Dudley would appear to have been his lea-land, pasture or open land.

By a quirk, Dudley's castle has always been in Staffordshire, although for centuries the town itself had been in Worcestershire, a small, pink blob in the surrounding green of Staffordshire in our early school atlases. Now, although the postal address is a pale "West Midlands", to all in the region Dudley stands firmly and proudly in "The Black Country". No longer is Dudley soot-soiled, supporting down-at-heel, oppressed labourers. By determination and endeavour her citizens and municipal officers have raised the town to one of beauty and interest, to the extent of being described elsewhere as "Queen of the Black Country". It grew up around the castle mound and there seem to be no really old buildings, Dudley developing mainly in the 18th and 19th centuries. The census of 1931 gives a population of 59,579. Fifty years later, 299,351 people lived in the enlarged borough. The latest figure is 301,047 inhabitants.

Powerful families have lived in and ruled the town — from the de Somerys in the 12th century to the de Suttons and their descendant, John Dudley, who became Duke of Northumberland. Right up to modern times, of course, the Earls of Dudley (the Ward family), have been landowners and industrialists, creating wealth and keeping a keen eye on the town. After the great fire of 1750, the Earls left the castle and resided at Himley Hall. In recent times the present Earl has resided elsewhere and the Hall has become municipally owned.

Dudley has always been a resourceful town with weekly markets and fairs at varying intervals, yet it did not achieve municipal borough status until 1865 and County Borough level until 1889. Upon becoming a Metropolitan Borough in 1974, Dudley adopted a new emblem which indicated forward-looking co-operation and trust between the Local Authority, commerce and industry.

For the purposes of this book, we have "blurred the edges" of the map a little to include photographic gems just outside the tight confines of the earlier Dudley, and maybe Halesowen and Stourbridge will yet feature in our future books of "Memories".

Standard 1, Colley Lane Council School (Boys), 1910.

BEGINNINGS

During our research we were constantly seeing the results of a well-organised education system in Dudley. Schools were buzzing with activity. Children with notepads, clipboards and simple cameras were inspecting, logging, sketching and filming local sites of interest. In all the libraries we visited the children's sections were so well supported that we are confident that tomorrow's generation will be well-read and capable of clear, convincing argument.

The Grammar School in Dudley was founded in the fourth year of Queen Elizabeth I's reign (1562). The present buildings were erected in 1898, opened a year later and considerably enlarged in 1909.

Well-sited in Priory Road, the Girls' High School (now The Dudley School) was opened in 1910, had a Kindergarten Department for juniors and a special department to prepare girls for the universities. High School fees at this time were 12 guineas (£12.60) per term.

Our Dennis Moore's father, born in Hayseech in 1899, received his early education at the old "Iron School" at the junction of Halesowen Road and Saltwells Road.

Today's education service is ensuring that industrial training, organised through the Local Authority, is geared to the growth industries.

27 E(G) P 28391 D, JULY 1925

DUDLEY EDUCATION COMMITTEE

Head Teacher
School

Communications on Different Subjects should form Separate Letters to the Office.

23/12/1925

John Evans, of 73 Cawney Hill, has been a scholar in this School since 12: 4: 20. He has reached the Seventh Standard.

During the two years that I have known him I have always found him to be a quiet, well-behaved boy. He attended carefully to his lessons & was always painstaking. He proved himself a most willing boy both inside school and in connection with outdoor games.

I consider him to be a boy who will prove reliable & persevering in his work.

Signed: H. Evans, Hd Teacher.

CERTIFIED COPY of an ENTRY of BIRTH.

SUPPLIED AT THE SPECIAL FEE OF 6d. APPLICABLE IN CERTAIN STATUTORY CASES.

THIS CERTIFICATE IS ISSUED FOR THE PURPOSES OF ....Unemployment....
and for NO OTHER USE OR PURPOSES WHATEVER.

The Registration Officer must state here statutory purposes for which the Certificate is issued in the terms in which they are described in printed Form of Requisition.

Registration District .... DUDLEY.

1913   BIRTH in the Sub-District of ....Tipton.... in the County of ....Stafford....

No.	When and where born	Name (if any)	Sex	Name and Surname of Father	Name and Maiden Surname of Mother	Rank or Profession of Father	Signature, Description and Residence of Informant	When Registered	Signature of Registrar	Baptismal Name if added after Registration of Birth
206	Nineteenth August 1913 5 High Street U.D.	Dora Irene	Girl	John Moore	Alice Moore formerly Roche	Colliery Winding Engine Driver	Alice Moore Mother 5 High Street Tipton	Thirtieth September 1913	Charles Asher Registrar	

I hereby certify that the above is a true Copy of an Entry of Birth in a Register Book in my custody.

Witness my hand this 1st day of August 1930.

Superintendent Registrar.

[NOTE.—The word "Superintendent" to be struck out when Certificate is given by the Registrar.]

Mount Pleasant
Council School,
Quarry Bank,
1926.

Brook Street
Mixed School,
Wordsley,
1937.

Form 1A, Dudley
Grammar School,
1948.

Providence Methodist Church, Colley Gate, Sunday School Anniversary, 1955.

First day of the new school year at Holly Hall School, 1960.

Pupils at Saltwells Secondary Modern School, (the old "Iron School"), Saltwells Road/Halesowen Road, 1960.

Dancing around the maypole in The Coppice, Pensnett, 1963.

'We can hear ourselves think'

WORDSLEY Toddlers' Tufty Club is now split into a road safety club and a play-group for the under-threes, and the organiser Mrs. Dorothy Cartwright happily reported after this month's meeting: "We can now hear ourselves think!"

When the club opened three months ago there was such a crush that some toddlers and their mothers could not even get into the main upstairs room of the Community Centre. Last month the turn-out was even greater so it was decided to split the club into two groups. 1967

Upper 6th Form, Sir
Gilbert Claughton
Grammar Technical
School, 1964.

Prize winners in the
Children's Scrapbook
Competition at
Brierley Hill
Children's Library,
April 1965.

MAIDENSBRIDGE
1984-1985

Trinity School, Halesowen Road, Cradley Heath, February 1971.

THEY ALSO SERVE

The St John Ambulance Association was formed in the town in 1892. By 1904 a new lecture-room and headquarters were in being near the Central Fire Station where a horse-drawn ambulance was kept in case of serious accidents. It had 300 members by 1931.

In 1871, as a result of a handsome endowment by a local benefactor, Joseph Guest, the former Blind Asylum in Tipton Road was modified to become the aptly-named Guest Hospital which has served the public so well right up to the present day.

The Police Force of 1925 consisted of a Chief Constable, 3 Inspectors, 6 sergeants and 45 constables, operating from the police station in Priory Street. The convenient telephone number was Dudley 2222.

A public library and art school were established in 1884 at the corner of Priory Street and St James's Road, and the present Central Library started life in 1909. Now some 800,000 books are in stock, together with audio-tapes, video-tapes and records. The Schools Library Service provides books, project materials and advice for some 170 schools in the borough. The staff at the Central and Branch libraries that we have visited have all been most helpful and courteous.

Netherton Section, Worcestershire Constabulary, 1908.

Dudley Fire Engine, 1901.

solation Hospital, Merry Hill, Quarry Bank, c. 1898.

AFS (Auxiliary Fire Service), Dudley, Spring 1945.

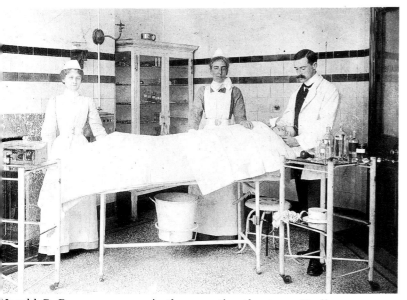

Harold C. Brown, surgeon, in the operating theatre at Dudley
Guest Hospital, c. 1902.

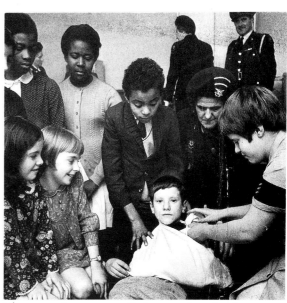

New recruits are enrolled as cadets in the
British Red Cross Society at Dudley Guest
Hospital, 3rd December 1968.

Coseley Nursing Division, St John Ambulance, 1954.

Miss E.A.M. Whitehouse, MBE, is presented with a bouquet after retiring from the British Red Cross, Coseley, 30th May 1973.

Meals on wheels, courtesy of the WVS (now WRVS), St John's Street, Netherton, 4th August 1961.

The Earl of Dudley, Regional Commissioner for Civil Defence, March 1942.

ARP (Air Raid Precautions) Wardens, Brierley Hill, 5th April 1939.

Emergency feeding exercise, Brierley Hill, 28th September 1955.

13

Arrival of the procession at Brockmoor Church for the unveiling of additional names on the War Memorial, 8th October 1950.

Brierley Hill Remembrance Sunday Parade approaching St Michael's Church, 1956.

British Legion Parade at Kingswinford, 28th June 1958.

SHORT LIFE 1967

Three days after a fence had been erected outside the 7th Dudley Scout Group's new headquarters in Watsons Green Road, Dudley, a vehicle backed into the drive and demolished two of the posts, causing damage amounting to £7 10s.

Mr. F. E. Davies, Group Scout Leader said this week that the scouts had spent three months producing a show to raise the £50 for the fence.

Soon after it was erected two corner posts were demolished by an unknown vehicle.

"Apparently someone delivering to a bakery next door was to blame," said Mr. Davies.

The bakery are making enquiries amongst their drivers but so far no one has come forward.

The scouts are now thinking of ways to raise the £7 10s. to repair the fence.

Brownies welcome the Queen on her visit to Rowley Regis, 23rd April 1957.

15

"He Can Break Every Fetter"

Dudley Citadel Band, Salvation Army, 1937.

16

EVENTS

Throughout the years, Dudley has been favoured with visits by members of the Royal Family and the oft-quoted "Queen Elizabeth I slept here" is a fact for she did indeed stay at Dudley Castle in 1575.

From about 1850, annual three-day Whitsuntide Fairs had been held in the castle grounds, with an unprecedented 20,000 or so people enjoying the festivities in 1916. The carnival of 1929 produced a gross income of £5,000 but a similar event in the following year saw a reduction in income of £1,500 due to deterioration in local trade and a broadly repetitive programme of events. Netherton's carnival in the same year suffered from poor weather, yet £403 was still raised for local charities.

The Dudley Housing Committee was able to announce that in 1930 the 2,000th council house had been erected and let.

Later that year, to provide an additional 54 beds, and at a cost of £25,000, a newly-erected wing of the Guest Hospital was opened by Princess Mary, later to become the Princess Royal of the day.

It was on 19th May 1939 that the Mayor, Ald A. Elliott Young, laid the foundation stone of the Police Station on the corner of New Street and Tower Street.

Because of declining traffic Dudley railway station closed in 1964, but a Freightliner Depot, the first in the Midlands, opened in November 1967 on the same site. Problems occurred and, after a reprieve until 1983, it closed soon afterwards.

Baggeridge Colliery opened in 1905, and eventually achieved the distinction of being the last colliery in the Black Country still working. It closed on 1st March 1968.

Planned in 1971 as a £1¾ million project, the Trident Shopping Centre opened on 11th September 1973, thus adding another dimension to Dudley's central shopping area.

Having occupied its somewhat sombre premises in Wolverhampton Street since 1909, the Post Office moved to a modern building in the Market Place in April 1986.

A spell in the sunshine, c. 1895. Three-day charity fetes were held in the grounds of Dudley Castle from 1850 until the First World War.

Edward, Prince of Wales, visits Dudley, 13th June 1923.

The Duke and Duchess of York (now the Queen Mother) visit Dudley Guest Hospital in aid of the £10,000 appeal, 4th June 1925.

St Aidan's Mission Mother's Union Meeting, Daisy Bank, 1924.

Ladies' outing from Green's Foundry, Coseley, c. 1928.

Opening of Dudley Town Hall by the Prime Minister, Rt. Hon. Stanley Baldwin, 16th October 1928.

Opening of Fisher Street Bus Station, October 1952.

Opening of Kingswinford Library, Market Street, 11th December 1955.

Opening of the Civic Suite, Brierley Hill, by the Chairman of the Urban District Council, Mrs M.J. Pargeter, 21st September 1957.

Queen Elizabeth II walks to the Council House with the Mayor, Coun. Danks, 24th April 1957.

22

Training College Rag Day, Market
Place, 12th May 1956.

Wall Heath Fete, 22nd August 1959.

Sale of Work, Hill Street Methodist
Church, Brierley Hill, 1964.

Members of the Dudley Canal Tunnel Preservation Society filmed for ATV's "Midland Montage", 5th March 1964.

Opening of Churchill Precinct by Lord Cobham, Lord Lieutenant of Worcestershire, 9th September 1969.

25

Coseley Carnival Tableau, 1975.

The three youngest daughters of the Earl and Countess of Dudley are christened together, 24th June 1970. The Countess, former film star Maureen Swanson, appeared in such films as "Moulin Rouge", "A Town Like Alice" and "The Spanish Gardener".

Queen Elizabeth II Silver Jubilee Street Party, Tower Road, Tividale, 7th June 1977.

ON THE MOVE

Placed as it is within an industrial region and so far away from sea-ports as it is possible to get, it was essential that Dudley should take to heart the early task of providing a good communications system. Accordingly, a network of canals with small branches or basins running up to the numerous factories facilitated the transport of raw materials and coal to those factories and foundries and likewise hauled away the finished products. Tipton is renowned for its extensive canal system. The Dudley Canal Tunnel, nearly two miles long, was built in 1792, connecting the Birmingham Canal to the Stourbridge Canal. An extension from the Castle Mill basin to right under the Wrens Nest is 1,227 yards long.

On 1st May 1850, a railway was opened from Dudley to Walsall and later, in March 1878, the GWR (Great Western Railway) formally began passenger services from Dudley to Old Hill and from Old Hill to Halesowen.

Steam trams began to run from Dudley to Birmingham in 1885 and by 1900 electric trams began service to Cradley Heath, a system which lasted some nine years. Trolley buses took over eventually, to be superseded by our present-day buses.

With the construction of the motorways and with Dudley's easy access to them and to the airports at Birmingham and Halfpenny Green, the town finds itself at the hub of a fine transport system, ideal for the movement of goods in and out and for the conveyance of passengers. Things have come a long way since the formation of the Dudley Bicycle Club in 1878!

Steam Tram and Engine, Tipton Road, 1901.

Open top bogie
electric tramcar,
Dudley Station
terminus, 1902.

Tramway and Motor
Express, Tipton
Road, Dudley, 1915.
The load-bearing
trailer was only used
during the first World
War.

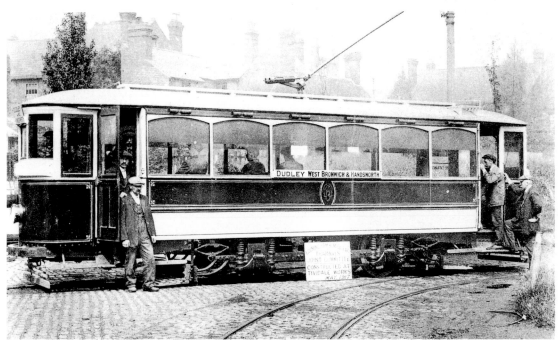

Prototype "Tividale"
tramcar, Tividale
Works, 1917.

The last tram on the Dudley to Stourbridge route, March 1930.

Birmingham Corporation tramcar, Boat Inn, Dudley Road East, Tividale, 23rd August 1939.

Castle Hill, August 1938.

Himley Road, 5th March 1959.

27th July 198

Stone Street, 1966. This trolleybus ran until 5th March 1967. On the evening of that day it went to Don Everall's scrapyard, Bilston Road, Wolverhampton. A scrap-merchant collected it as soon as it arrived and by nightfall it had been transferred to Station Garage, Bilston for storage. Acquired by a Walsall company, by 19th March 1967 it had been dismantled.

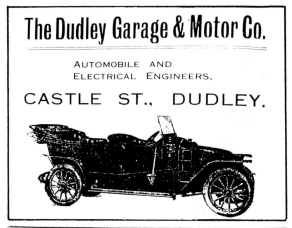

ADVICE TO MOTORISTS

"Anticipate the clots!"
MARCH 1968

It was a red-letter day for 18-year-old Janice Tapako, forecourt salesgirl at Brettell Lane Service Station, when Derek Roy drove up in his Hudson Customline and asked: "Fill her up—I'm celebrating the $\frac{3}{4}$d. off petrol!"

Derek Roy, better-known to hundreds of Brierley Hill children as Buttons since his performances at the Dudley Hippodrome's pantomime "Cinderella," sheltered from the driving rain in the beautifully-equipped office of this new Station.

"I may be funny on the stage," exclaimed the Doctor of Fun, "but the minute I'm behind a wheel the comedy is dropped. Driving is a serious business these days." The star who has triumphed in every sphere from radio to stage had good advice for road users—"Anticipate the clots," he warned, "I've managed to develop a sixth sense over the years and have found that it is impossible to drive by rule of thumb."

Derek Roy.

Withymoor Goods Station, Northfield Road, Netherton, 1962.

LMS Class 8F 2-8-0 No. 48514 travels through Dudley Port (Low Level) Station, 25th July 1959.

Members of the South Staffs branches of the Workers Education Association travel through the Dudley Tunnel, October 1963.

Bicycle Proficiency Test
Finalists, Buckpool School,
Hawbush, Brierley Hill, 1974.

AT WORK

Near at hand were all the essentials for iron-smelting — the ironstone itself, limestone, fireclay for furnace lining and one of the thickest coal-seams in Britain. Earlier smelters had consumed local forests at an alarming rate in order to fuel their furnaces, but in the seventeenth century the aptly named Dud Dudley discovered that coal could do the job better, so the woodlands were conserved and the coal industry flourished alongside that of iron. Nails, anchors and chains, together with anvils and vices were produced in large quantities. Locally brewed beers and stouts slaked the thirsts of the iron-workers.

Later, motor cars at Beans Industries provided transport for the growing population and for international competitions. Even GPO postboxes were made in the town.

Julia Hanson & Sons Ltd., the only brewery to bear a lady's name, was established in 1847 and Teddy Gray had earlier set up his sweet factory in 1826. Alfred Preedy gave up his naval career and in 1869 began a retail tobacco shop which developed into the Alfred Preedy & Sons Ltd chain.

Commerce has flourished in the capable hands of solicitors, estate agents, travel agents, insurance companies, bankers and so many others.

Princes End Colliery, Tipton, c. 1890.

Miners and pit sinkers, The Crooked House, Himley, 1921.

Clay Pit, Dibdale Lane, Lower Gornal, c. 1910.

Claymining, Amblecote Road, Brierley Hill, 1970. The three ponies used in the mine were taken above ground after each day's work.

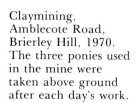

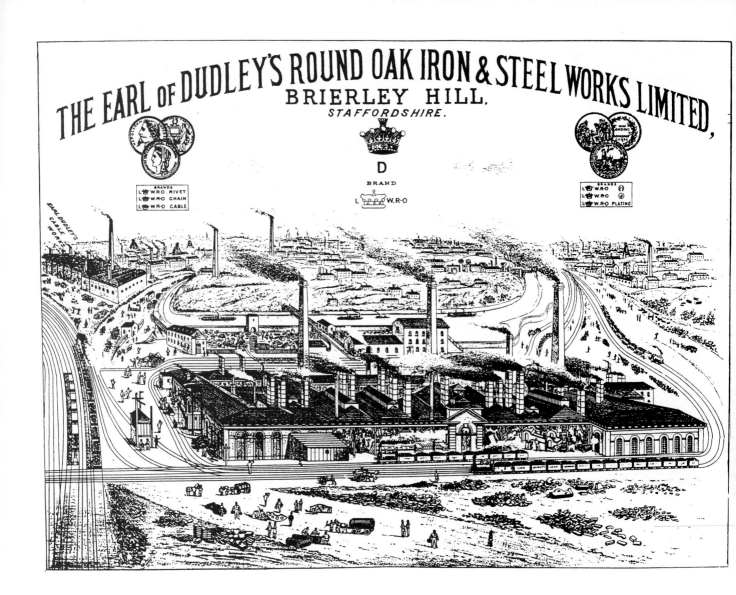

THE EARL of DUDLEY'S ROUND OAK IRON & STEEL WORKS LIMITED,
BRIERLEY HILL.
STAFFORDSHIRE.

ROUND OAK STEEL WORKS LTD
CONSTRUCTIONAL DEPT
Feb. 24. 1938.

A team of twenty horses pulls the anchor for the Titanic from Hingley's, Netherton, to Dudley Port Station, 1911. Further anchors were made by Hingley's for the liners Queen Mary and Queen Elizabeth.

Lloyds British Testing Co. Ltd., Proving House, Netherton, c. 1929.

Dudley Bucket and Fender Co-operative, Charlotte
Street, 1901.

Spotwelders leave British Federal Welder, Castle Mill Works, en route to Pressed Steel Co., 1938. The left foreground building and the centre background building housed the original mill which provided power for Dudley Castle.

41

A Babcock and Wilcox gathering for the company magazine, New Birmingham Road, 1948.

Steel process vessels for a Teesside oil tanker under construction. Danks Gowerton, Netherton, 17th May 1974.

BALMORAL CASTLE

18th October, 1982

Dear Mr. McKinGr,

It must have been enormously satisfying for you to see the successful raising of the Mary Rose with the cradle, designed and produced by your firm, playing such a prominent part. I am only too well aware of the skill and considerable amount of work that must have gone into making it work so well on the day and I would be most grateful if you could pass on my thanks to all those involved.

Yours sincerely

Charles

Prince Charles' letter to Babcock Construction (previously Babcock and Wilcox).

Molten metal being poured from a cupola. Thomas Dudley Ltd., New Birmingham Road, celebrated their Golden Jubilee in 1970.

50th Anniversary celebrations (complete with company cat!), British Federal Welder & Machine Company, Castle Mill Works, 1980.

High Street, Dudley, 1897.

Joseph Smith outside his leather and shoe shop, 6 Castle Street, Dudley, c. 1915.

King Street, Dudley, 1912.

TEAS. THE TEAS.
BON BON
CAFE
HOT LUNCHEONS DAILY

245, CASTLE STREET
DUDLEY 1925

J.A. Adams' shop, Furlong Lane,
Colley Gate, 1933.

High Street, Dudley, 1957.

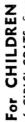

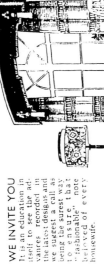

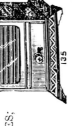

Mrs Winchurch at the door of her shop — the last remaining building in the
redevelopment area, Flood Street, June 1963.

Market Place, looking towards St Edmund's Church, July 1963.

Jim Hughes at work inside his boot and shoe repair shop, 17th October 1979. See below.

A familiar sight to Midlanders was this wooden shed, which acted for over 30 years as a cobbler's workshop, on the junction of Birmingham New Road and Sedgley Road, Woodsetton.

Black Country "Tatters", Ocker Hill, Tipton, May 1971.

A special small team of pie-makers worked all day to produce this monster 60lb pork pie at Palethorpe's, Dudley Port, 10th November 1958.

Marsh & Baxter's new meat and sausage room, Brierley Hill, 1st April 1959.

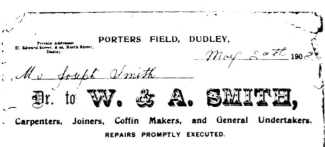

PORTERS FIELD, DUDLEY,

Private Address:
17, Edward Street, & 64, North Street,
Dudley.

May 20th 1902

Mr Joseph Smith

Dr. to W. & A. SMITH,

Carpenters, Joiners, Coffin Makers, and General Undertakers.

REPAIRS PROMPTLY EXECUTED.

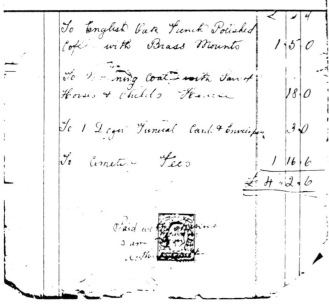

Test sampling a brew at Julia Hanson's Brewery, Upper High Street, Dudley, 1961.

AT PLAY

For workers to relax at the end of a hard day's work and at weekends to take up some more vigorous form of leisure is typical of industrial towns like Dudley.

As far back as 1837 horse-racing began near Castle Hill and lasted there for some eleven years.

William Perry, the famous bare-fisted "Tipton Slasher", had a great following and became Boxing Champion of England from 1850 to 1857.

The year 1880 appears an important one for Dudley's swimmers when a Men's Club was formed. In 1885 a Ladies' section followed. The Public Baths in Blower's Green Road were opened on 23rd August 1880 and the New Corporation Baths followed on 19th September 1928 just after the Council had approved mixed bathing.

Throughout the years the Sports Editions of local newspapers show bowls, football, rugby and cricket leagues in profusion, indicating the tremendous support of the public.

The Dudley Golf Club's new course at Oakham was opened for play in April 1927, when a full year's subscription for men was £5 and for ladies £2.

By the late 1930's Dudley's cinemas were The Regent Picture House, The Criterion, The Empire, The Castle and The Scala. Perhaps the cinema name that is most evocative of a pleasant Saturday night out is The Cosy (at Coseley), which sadly closed in 1957.

During the winters of the early 1930's a young man could take his partner for dancing on Mondays and Saturdays to the Palais de Danse in the Public Hall, Wolverhampton Street.

The Opera House, known as The Front Door of Dudley, opened in Castle Hill on 4th September 1889 with a performance of "The Mikado" by the D'Oyly Carte Opera Company. It was destroyed by fire on 1st November 1936.

Thanks to the advent of television sports coverage, snooker is enjoying a boost with snooker halls and leisure centres catering for the needs of hopeful champions.

Dudley Amateur Association F.C., 1908.

Darkhouse Chapel F.C., Coseley, 1926.

Dudley Town F.C. Birmingham League, 12th September 1953.

Quarry Bank Junior School F.C., 1962.

TO-NIGHTS TEAMS

Dudley Town		Wolverhampton Wanderers
SHIRTS: RED SHORTS: WHITE		SHIRTS: GOLD SHORTS: BLACK
STEVE POMROY	1	PAUL BRADSHAW
BEN BROWN (Capt.)	2	GEOFF PALMER
JEFF RUMJAHN	3	DEREK PARKIN
GARY MORTON	4	MICK MATTHEWS
PAUL PRIDGEON	5	JOE GALLAGHER
LIONEL MARTIN	6	COLIN BRAZIER
JOHN SMITH	7	ALAN BIRCH
NEIL CIVIL	8	WAYNE CLARKE
PAUL WILKINSON	9	MEL EVES
GARY FLEET	10	PETER DANIEL
GAVIN LANG	11	WILLIE CARR
IAN McPHEE	12	JOHN RICHARDS
MARK STANTON		BILL LIVINGSTONE

REFEREE: MR. D. W. CIVIL (BIRMINGHAM) 3/11/81

LINESMEN: MR. I. R. FULLER (RED FLAG)
MR. R. T. NEWELL (YELLOW FLAG)

uncan Edwards, Manchester United F.C. and English ternational Footballer, born on the Priory Estate, died a result of the Munich Air Disaster, February 1958, hen only 21.

Dudley Town F.C. play Wolves, 3rd November 1981.

55

Dudley Cricket Club, 29th June 1957.

Brierley Hill Police Cricket Club, 8th September 1969.

Dudley-Kingswinford R.F.C., 28th February 1959.

Tennis Team, Dudley Girls' High School, c. 1937.

Dudley's own Miss Dorothy Round, beats Miss Helen Jacobs (U.S.A.) in the Ladies' Singles Final at Wimbledon, 7th July 1934.

The 18th hole, Dudley Golf Course, Rowley Regis, 4th May 1964.

Dudley Grasshoppers Netball Team, 14th July 1978.

Opening of the Woodman Bowling Green, Dudley
Wood, 21st April 1956.

Jack Holden, Tipton Harriers, (No 73) came third in the 14th Annual Staffs County Championship 1939.

Judo Club Exhibition, Dudley Town Hall, 1956.

Finalists in the under-fifteens 200 yards sprint at Wordsley Scouts Sports Day, 20th September 1958.

A TOWN HONOURS "SLASHER"

8/7/49

THE Mayor of Tipton (Ald. W. E. Hampton) last night accepted, on behalf of the Corporation, an oil painting of the Tipton Slasher, pugilist champion of England, 1850-57.

The picture was presented by Mr. J. C. Fisher, an antique collector, who obtained it from Mrs. E. Harding, of Ocker Hill, Tipton.

Mrs. Harding's great-grandfather was a brother of The Slasher (whose real name was William Perry). She expressed a wish that the painting should remain in Tipton.

Many Tipton residents subscribed to have it restored. The name of the artist could not be deciphered.

Story of the ape

Mr. Fisher also obtained a stuffed ape from Mrs. Harding. The story was that it was one of the Slasher's sparring partners.

The Mayor related Perry's fights from 1836, when he defeated Ben Spilsbury at Oldbury, to his defeat by Tom Sayers in 1857.

Speaking of The Slasher's appearance, the Mayor said: "His face usually wore a kindly expression."

The picture is to be hung in Tipton Central Library.

Tom Langley, author of "The Tipton Slasher", autographs copies of his book at the launching ceremony at the Fountain Inn, Owen Street, Tipton, 18th July 1969.

1964

Cradley Heath Speedway Team receive the Speedway Star K.O. Cup after their win in Hull, November 1979.

Dudley's "It's a Knockout" squad, which took part in the BBC TV Series, 1979.

Opera House, Castle Hill, c. 1932.

THE HIPPODROME
DUDLEY
PROPRIETORS - - KENNEDY'S THEATRES LTD.

Joint Managing Directors ROBERT F. KENNEDY and MAURICE B. KENNEDY
House Manager ... ... PETER ROBINSON
Musical Director ... ... EDMUND WELCH
Publicity ... ... GEORGE BARTRAM
Stage Director ... ... JACK BENSON

Box Office open 10 a.m. to 9 p.m. Phone : 201811

PRICES OF ADMISSION (Including Tax)

	Monday to Friday	Saturday and Holidays
BOX SEATS	7/6	7/6
GRAND STALLS	5/-	5/6
STALLS	3/9	4/6
PIT STALLS	2/-	3/-
ROYAL CIRCLE	4/9	5/-
GRAND CIRCLE	3/3	4/-
CIRCLE	2/3	3/6
UPPER CIRCLE	1/-	1/6

Week Commencing Monday, September 15th, 1952

Twice Nightly at 6-15 and 8-30 :: Matinee Saturday 2-30

1. **OVERTURE**

2. **THE LONSDALE SISTERS**
   "Rhythm"

3. **LORRAINE**
   The Singing Cartoonist

4. **The Sensational AERIAL KENWAYS**

5. **ARCHIE ELRAY and COMPANY**
   in Ventriloquial Scena

6. **THE GREAT CINGALEE**
   and His Company of Skilled Mystifiers
   The "Silent Man of Mystery" in Oriental Magic

7. **INTERVAL**

8. **THE LONSDALE SISTERS**

9. **JIMMIE ELLIOTT**
   Famous Animal Mimic of Radio

10. **MACKENZIE REID & DOROTHY**
    Ace Accordionists

11. BERNARD DELFONT presents

STAN LAUREL and OLIVER HARDY

in

"A SPOT OF TROUBLE"

A comedy sketch in two scenes

Locale : A small town in the U.S.A.

1. .... **Waiting room at the Railway Station**

2. .... **The Chief of Police's living room**

Cast :

Officer (*a small town cop with a mind smaller than the town*)

LESLIE SPURLING

Chief of Police .... KENNETH HENRY

Two Gentlemen en route .... **STAN LAUREL**
and **OLIVER HARDY**

NATIONAL ANTHEM

Chocolates and Cigarettes may be obtained from the kiosks

14th October 1952.

HIPPODROME

MONDAY OCTOBER 13th NIGHTLY 6.15 TWICE NIGHTLY 8.30

14th BIRTHDAY WEEK.

HARRY PETER
SECOMBE SELLERS SEMPRINI

ELEANOR TRIO DOLORES & LEONARDO

LACY TROUPE BOB HATCH

KAREN LESLIE DANDY
GREER WELCH BROTHERS

THIS WEEK AT 6.15 & 8.30 RECORD ROUNDABOUT FEATURING EDDIE CALVERT AND ALL STAR COMPANY

Coseley Brass Band (before they had uniforms) play at a hospital day, near Roseville Square, Coseley, c. 1925. The conductor was Noah Insley.

Cradley Heath & District Choral Society, 1950.

Brierley Hill Amateur Operatic Society's production of "Maid of the Mountains", 1962.

Odeon Cinema, Dudley, 1937.

66

James Whale, 14th December 1933.

The Midlands' first
drive-in movie "E.T." is
shown in a car park at
the Merry Hill Centre,
near Dudley, 9th
October 1988.

One of the most famous "Dames" in the history of pantomime, Clarkson Rose.

DUDLEY CHARACTERS

Dolly Allen, one of the stars of "The Black Country Night Out" team.

TV Personality Sue Lawley.

Comedian Lenny Henry.

BILLY DAINTY

One of the best-loved characters ever to emerge from the Black Country, Billy was born in Wolverhampton Street, Dudley, on 22nd February 1927. He became a superb eccentric dancer and comedian, appearing in theatres throughout the U.K. and moving into television via "Sunday Night at the Palladium". He died on 19th November 1986.

Sister Betty, with Billy in 1941.

Behind a freshly painted grocery shop in Wolverhampton Street, Dudley, lies an unusual and flourishing business run by two sisters, and patronised by the Royal Kennels at Sandringham, huntsmen, leading dog breeders, and zoological societies throughout the country.

The business, which has been in existence for over 50 years, has been in the news from time to time whenever it has been announced that a Dudley dog has been sent to one of the zoos to act as foster mother to perhaps tiger or leapard cubs.

Hooper Brothers (Canine Foster Specialists) have from time to time supplied most of the leading zoos including Regents Park,

Whipsnade, Bristol, Glasgow, and the local zoo with dogs to act as foster mothers.

At the moment, "Maggie," a mongrel terrier, normally housed at Wolverhampton Street, is away at London Zoo looking after two tiger cubs. She was hurried to London after the tigress had lost interest in her offspring soon after their birth

BROKE RECORD

"Maggie," however, is only the latest example of the work of these Dudley dogs. It may be remembered about five years ago that "Nannie," another local foster mother, broke a 35 years record at Regents Park Zoo when

she reared two leapard cubs.

The business, at present in the hands of Mrs. Florence Dainty and Mrs. Ada Preece, was taken over by the two sisters after the death of their father.

He founded the concern with his brother after some years with Birmingham Police Force during which time his duties included the care of dogs.

Although running the kennels, dealing with the demands from all their various clients, and the occasional emergency call from a zoo, keeps both sisters busy they find time for spare time summer occupations. Both sisters act as swimming instructresses, Mrs. Dainty at West Bromwich, and her sister at Birmingham. 1951

Despite the poster, that is Billy on the left! His close friend Roy Hudd, along with Jimmy Cricket, organised a tribute to him at the Grand Theatre, Wolverhampton on 29th January 1989.

Billy's grandmother and mother.

THE TOWN CENTRE

A fine downhill sweep from St. Thomas's (Top Church) takes us along a High Street once graced by the impressive store of F.W. Cook Ltd (established in 1819), the Co-operative Emporium, William Cranage's Cafe (which offered a smoking lounge in addition to a stylish dining room) and the Sunshine Laundry at number 50 where flannel trousers could be cleaned for 1/3d (6½ p), riding breeches for 2/6d (12½ p) and overcoats for 5/-(25p). Carry on into the wide Market Place where the Dudley Arms Hotel was sited, a welcoming spot for the traveller and local alike and a modest conference centre for numerous committees and trade societies. Where the well-known fountain of 1867 still stands, the Old Town Hall occupied the site prior to demolition in 1860.

The colourful and cheerful noise of the Market Place is left behind as the approach is made to St. Edmund's Church in Castle Street which was built in 1722, and towards the statue of William, Earl of Dudley, unveiled by his widow, Georgina, on 25th April 1888 in remembrance of the many benefits he had conferred on the town and district. Going down Castle Hill we arrive at the Zoo (in the Castle grounds) which was opened in May 1937 and where the curved entrance gates, considered frankly modern at that time, are now a listed building.

Nearer to the town centre, much of Hall Street has been given over to the Churchill Precinct, but a short walk along the rest of Hall Street is the sad, almost theatrical shell of the Dudley Co-operative Society Head Office at Waddam's Pool, with the adjoining bakery in North Street, empty and forlorn but still displaying a certain style.

Throughout its length, Wolverhampton Street has some magnificent buildings which house the professions and the business offices.

St James's Road, c. 1900.

71

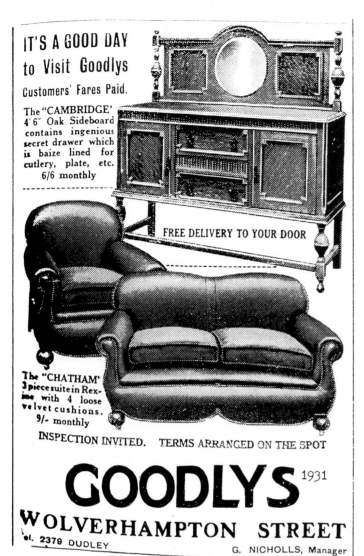

Priory Street, looking towards Wolverhampton Street, c. 1898.

Inhedge, c. 1912.

A Porter's Field house and shop, converted to a menagerie, 1936.

Dudley was one of the towns represented in the BBC Midlands' TV series "Know Your Place". Alton who hosted the programme (as well as acting as scriptwriter and researcher) toured most of the West Bromwich Building Society offices with copies of his first book based on the series. Here he stands, second right, outside Stone Street branch, 15th September 1982.

Seven Stars Inn, High Street/Market Place, 21st October 1949.

74   The Market Place, 5th November 1946.

Campbell Street decorated for the Coronation, June 1953.

Ednam Restaurant, Fisher Street, 1956.

The Empire, Hall Street, 1959.

High Street, June 1963, from Top Church down towards the Market Place during the Training College Rag Day.

The Fountain, Market Place, c. 1884.

OUT AND ABOUT

This is where we tear around the edges of our map and tack on a few odd corners of the district where we have found items of charm and interest. We enter into no controversies as to what is and what is not now "Dudley".

In the 10th century, Kingswinford was merely Swinford, a swine's ford, and the prefix "King" was added to distinguish between other Swinfords. It still has its village green, pub and row of cottages.

Gornal, consisting of Upper and Lower Gornal and Gornal Wood, was recorded in the 15th century as Guarnell or Gwarnell (derived from "cwerne" or "quern" — the ancient names for a mill). Oddly, there is no record of a windmill there before that time as, originally, all mills were hand-mills.

In the Domesday Book (1086), and later, Himley appears as Himelie, having origins in hymele, the hop plant. Sadly, no hops grow on its sheltered lands now. There is a model village near to Himley Hall and Park.

Tipton was once in hunting country. It might well have derived its name from St. Tibbe who died in 696.

Mushroom Green, near Quarry Bank, has its small craft chain-shop, whilst there are nature reserves at the Wrens Nest, Saltwells and Cotwall End. A lower town, in relation to its neighbours, has given us the name Netherton.

Himley Hall, 1982, once the home of the Earls of Dudley.

Workmen laying a new water main in Oakeywell Street struck a coal seam just below the road surface, 19th October 1951.

Burton Road, Dudley, c. 1928.

The Broadway,
Dudley, 1937.

Bull Ring. Sedgley,
c. 1900.

Children from the
Priory Estate visit
the Wrens Nest,
8th April 1964.

Black Country programme

THE long awaited Black
Country radio programme
gets under way on Sunday after-
noon when regular broadcasts
commence from BBC Radio Birmingham.

Black Country writer, poet
and humorist Harry Harrison
will be doing a regular spot,
and pigeon expert, Bill Cattell,
of the New Inn, Coseley, will
cover the local racing scene.
Folk singer, Jean Burns, will be
a resident guest on the programme.

Mr. Harrison says: "The
Black Country has a rare wealth
of talent and history. This programme should blow a little
fresh air that could have
tremendous potential for the
future of the region."

1972

Removal of drinking fountain and memorial, Stourbridge Road, Woodside, April 1954.

46/48 Garrett Street, Hart's Hill, 1954.

Rocks Hill, Brierley Hill, 28th July 1955.

Opening of Brierley Hill Civic Hall, 11th May 1962.

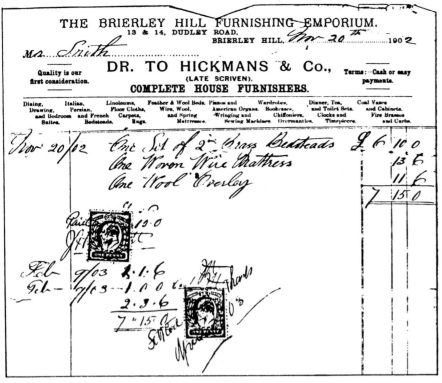

High Street, Cradley Heath, c. 1910.

Women's Bright
Hour Class,
Providence
Methodist Church,
Colley Gate, 1929.

Flames leap from
the blazing stand
at Cradley Heath
Speedway Stadium,
October 1977.

Stone laying ceremony,
Providence Methodist Church,
Colley Gate, 30th June 1962.

PROVIDENCE METHODIST CHURCH
COLLEY GATE

★

B.B.C.
PEOPLE'S SERVICE

SUNDAY, APRIL 20th, 1969

Preacher:
Rev. Dr. WM. STRAWSON, M.Th.

Theme:
"WORSHIP IS LIVING"

Assisted by Rev. R. R. GIFFARD

Lining up for Mary Ann Roe's home-brewed ale, The White Swan Inn, Baptist End, Netherton, c. 1910.

The Old Swan Inn, Halesowen Road, Netherton, February 1957. It was known affectionately as "Ma Pardoe's".

An ox-roast at Netherton Cricket Club Gala, 30th May 1955.

The Secretary of British Waterways Board, Trevor Luckcuck, re-opens the Netherton Tunnel after restoration, 18th April 1984.

Mary Ann Rushton's general store, High Street, Kingswinford, 1902.

The demolition of Dawley Brook Bridge, Kingswinford, April 1956. The bridge once carried the Ashwood-Pensnett railway line.

The Old Court House Inn, High Street, Kingswinford, c. 1903.

Peacock Inn, Wordsley, c. 1900.

Rear of Parker Place, Tipton, July 1971.

Looking towards the junction of Burnt Tree Road and Tividale Road (on the right), c. 1925. This is now the site of Burnt

Owen Street, Tipton, 1951.

Ocker Hill Junior School,
Gospel Oak Road, Tipton,
just prior to demolition.
4th March 1970.

Unromantic . . .

MY sister-in-law and
her daughter lived
next door to us, and every
time there was a raid they
used to join us in our shelter.

The daughter was married
on August 17, 1940, and as
usual the sirens went, so
into the shelter the bride
and groom came with us.

In fact, they spent their
nights in the shelter for a
whole week. What a honey-
moon!—MRS. S. FARRING-
TON, 8 Queens Avenue, Tividale, Tipton.

A Tipton aqueduct is
to be transformed to look
more like its old self.

The Ryland Aqueduct —
carrying a canal across the
main Dudley Port road — is
just a square looking concrete
structure at the moment.

But it was a traditional
aqueduct with archways.

Now Sandwell Council
experts have come up with an
idea is to paint archways onto
the aqueduct below silhouettes
in railings of two canal barges.

"We are trying to re-create
the old aqueduct in a highly
stylised version," said a
spokesman for the planning
department's re-generation
and environment section.

The hope is to carry out the
work after waterproofing of the
aqueduct in September.

The project was given planning permission yesterday by
the Black Country Development Corporation subject to
more talks with the council.

"Our architects will be
liaising with the council's on
the final appearance," said
development control planner,
Mr Clive Dutton.

The project follows the re-
painting of a railway bridge
over Bloomfield Road, Tipton,
like a piano keyboard — with
the notes of Glenn Miller's
classic Chattanooga Choo-Choo
welded to the handrail along
the top. 14.4.1989

Patent COOLMORE DURABLE ROOFING.

Waterproof, Dustproof, Stormproof and Fireproof. Not affected by climate. Ensures equable Temperature, and thus produces healthier dwellings.

NO REPAIRS REQUIRED.

All necessary information, together with Samples, Estimates, &c., on application to

J. H. Cartwright, Lawley Street, Dudley,

SOLE AGENT FOR DUDLEY AND DISTRICT.

Coolmore Patent Roofs or One, Two, and Three Layers Sheet Asphalte quoted for, on application, stating quantity required.
Quotations given for Circular Girder Roofs, Timber Work, and Covering complete.
Cheap and Durable Roofs for Foundries, Workshops, etc.

"Coolmore Durable" Damp Course, in rolls, 45 feet long, cut any width required. All work guaranteed.

THE DUDLEY GUARDIAN,

ESTABLISHED 1863.

Published every Saturday Morning at the Office, Newhall St. Dudley.

THE DUDLEY GUARDIAN is the only Newspaper printed and published in the large and important town of Dudley, containing upwards of 50,000 inhabitants, and circulates not only extensively in the town and neighbourhood, but also throughout the great Iron and Coal Districts of South Staffordshire and East Worcestershire (of which Dudley is the natural capital and centre), possessing a population of nearly Half a Million.

It forms a most advantageous medium for Advertisements relating to the Trade of the District, as well as the Announcements of Solicitors, Auctioneers, Estate Agents, Tradesmen, Insurance Companies, &c.; in fact, Advertisements which do not appear in the DUDLEY GUARDIAN must fail to come under the notice of a large and influential portion of the community.

PRINTING OF EVERY DESCRIPTION

IS EXECUTED AT THE

GUARDIAN OFFICE,

With the utmost punctuality and despatch, and upon the most moderate terms. Particular care has been exercised in selecting Types, Machinery, &c., the most suitable for

POSTING AND WINDOW BILLS,

For the rapid and efficient production of which, peculiar facilities are possessed by this Establishment.

Address Cards, Circulars, Billheads, Club Rules, Cheque Books (numbered and perforated, if required), &c., &c.

ENGRAVING (both Wood and Copperplate), in the first style of the Art, and upon the most reasonable terms.
LEDGERS, and all kinds of STATIONERY, made to Order, by competent Workmen, and at Town prices.
BOOKBINDING (plain or ornamental), equal to any House in the Trade.
MACHINE RULING (to any Pattern).

Observe the Address—

JOHN LUKIS, Printer, Newhall Street.

BRITISH HOMES

T. W. GOLDIE, Local Secretary.

Interesting Statistics concerning the

MOST LIBERAL SCHEME EVER DEVISED.
—— 1904

For the details of the figures which cram the the Report of

The British Homes Assurance Corporation

(A Report which spells SUCCESS on every page) we have no space, and the following summary must suffice :—

1. Proposals received for 1903 ... **Over £2,000,000**
2. The Funds have Increased in Six Years over ... **£240,000**
3. THE TOTAL INCOME is over **£100,000**
4. The aggregate amount that has been advanced to Certificate and Policy Holders since the Corporation began, is nearly **£500,000**
5. The Expenses have DECREASED 8—42 per cent.
6. Participating Life Policy Holders (General Section) 15 % Bonus.
7. Abstainers' Section, 20 per cent., and Endowment Certificate Holders, 12½ per cent., in addition to a Guaranteed Two per cent. Compound Interest.
8. Over 200 Editorial Notes of the Leading Papers of the day voluntarily given this year.
9. Over 8,000 rejoicing because they are possessors of their own Homes through joining this institution, at considerably less than what they were previously paying as rent, most having their lives insured, so that if they should die they leave their family free from Mortgage Charge or Encumbrance.

For Prospectus and Press Opinions apply to

T. W. Goldie, Waterloo House, Wellington Rd., Dudley

Deposits received at 3, 4 and 5%, withdrawable at any time as arranged.

Duraflex
Fashionable foot-room at reasonable cost

'DURAFLEX' TAB COURT
In black or brown supple glace kid. Wedge heel. 6 fitting; sizes 2 to 8. Price 55/9.

'DURAFLEX' 3-EYELET GIBSON
In black, brown or red unlined calf side. Wedge heel. 6 fitting; sizes 2 to 8. Price 55/9.

'DURAFLEX' COURT
in black, brown or grey calf. Louis heel, height 11". 6 fitting; sizes 2 to 8. Price 55/9.

Duraflex shoes are the wonderful answer to all women with footwear problems. They give you exact sizing and room for comfort—yes! But they give you fashion, too, at reasonable prices.

SEE THEM AT ALL

DUDLEY, WOLVERHAMPTON, BILSTON, WEST BROMWICH, WALSALL, BRIDGNORTH & OTHER MIDLAND TOWNS.

WE hope that all who visit the Zoo will spend happy and interesting hours there. We feel that the setting is unique, an ancient Castle, full of interest in itself, and representing stage by stage the history of our country; a wooded hillside, on which the Castle stands, adapted by experienced Architects so that the animals which are housed in the Zoological Gardens can be seen to the best advantage in beautiful modern settings, which in no way spoil or interfere with the charm of the great Castle itself.

WE hope that animal lovers will appreciate the comparative freedom and space which has been given to the animals, and we feel sure that this factor will greatly add to the enjoyment of visitors to the Society's grounds.

FURTHER, we feel that it should not be overlooked that the grounds stand in the middle of a vast industrial area. May we remind those who come from distant parts of the country or from abroad that within a few miles of Dudley there are factories and works turning out a greater variety of manufactured goods and raw materials of exceptional quality than in any other industrial area in the world. To those who are interested in industry, Chambers of Commerce and similar organisations will give full information, whereby a visit to the Society's grounds may easily serve to combine pleasure with a profitable business journey.

IN conclusion, we should like to thank all who have helped us in our new enterprise, and we trust that for many years people will enjoy the entertainment, refreshment and instruction which has been provided for them in the lovely Castle grounds.

6.5.37

Dudley

A. E. Marsh

Polar Bear pit, 19th May 1937.

SWAN RECOVERS AFTER FLYING INTO WIRES

Mr. Harry Hatch, head keeper at Dudley Zoo, was called out last night to the King Arthur Hotel, Priory-road, to tend a swan which had been injured when it flew into some telegraph wires.

The bird was taken to the zoo, where Mr. Hatch treated it for slight injuries to its head and neck, and today it was swimming on one of the zoo ponds.

The head keeper says he thought the swan would be all right in a few days, and when it was completely recovered it would be allowed to leave if it seemed inclind to do so.

A Bactrian camel, which originates from Russia, has been purchased through an Amsterdam dealer and will arrive at the zoo on Monday. 16.5.53

A section of the zoo's miniature railway, 2nd June 1938.

Three brown bear cubs, the first to be born at the zoo for several years, 25th March 1975.

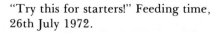

"Try this for starters!" Feeding time, 26th July 1972.

The ancient ruins of Dudley Castle and the modern additions that make Dudley Zoo stand out against the snow-covered background of Castle Hill. 5th March 1965.

THE BLACK COUNTRY MUSEUM

Preparing the site, Summer 1976.

The first passengers ride on the tram, 5th August 1980.

Black Country folk have an opportunity to travel back in time on a £50,000 tramcar system that has been brought back to life at Dudley.

The tramcar system is the Black Country Museum's latest attraction, and has already started drawing in the crowds since it opened yesterday.

It has the distinction of being Britain's only narrow-gauge tramway, and gives museum visitors a 600-yard ride from the museum's colliery site to the reconstructed village.

Although work started on the site in the mid-1970's, it was actually opened to the public in 1979. On 24th October 1985 HRH the Duke of Gloucester (on the right) formally opened the new entrance buildings.

The age of steam returns! 11th October 1987.

Sharon Rudge and Mark Tilt are married at the Bottle and Glass public house, 23rd July 1987. The wedding was part of the celebrations marking 150 years of the Registration Service.

ACKNOWLEDGEMENTS

(for providing anecdotes, memories, photographs, encouragement and numerous other favours)

Dolly Allen; Babcock Construction; George Bartram Press Relations; Birmingham Post & Mail Ltd.; Black Country Museum; Jim Boulton; Brierley Hill Library; British Federal Ltd.; Sylvia Butler; Dave Carpenter; Catherine & Charles Cartwright; John Cochrane; Joan Dainty; Dudley Libraries; Dudley Zoo & Castle; Bernard Francis; Noel Gay Ltd.; Goodyear Tyre & Rubber Co. (GB) Ltd.; Clive Hardy; Ethel Harper; Bryan Harris; Nora Harris; Hillcrest School & Community College; Robert Holmes; Roy Hudd; Clive Jaspar; Christine & Richard Jones; Sue Lawley; Michael Mensing; Philip Murphy; Ida Pearson; Betty Piddock; Rene & Eddie Preece; Victor Price; Winnie Price; Liz Rees; Saltwells Education Development Centre; Smethwick Library; David Smith; Murray Smith; Gordon Stretch; Wolverhampton & Dudley Breweries Ltd.; Wolverhampton Library; WRVS; Edna Yates.

Please forgive any possible omissions. Every effort has been made to include all organisations and individuals involved in the book.